To DEBBIE
May God bless
You Richly
Elder KAY

Be True
To What You Do:
Motivated to Serve
With Excellence

KAY F. BRUNDIDGE

Published by Claire Aldin Publications, LLC

Visit our website at www.clairealdin.com

Edited by: Shairon L. Taylor,

SLT Inspirations LLC

Cover Design: Sam Smith

ISBN-13: 978-0-9996840-2-3

Unless otherwise indicated, all scriptures are taken from the Holy Bible, King James Version, which is in the public domain.

ACKNOWLEDGEMENTS

To everyone who prayed and supported me throughout this journey, I thank you.

To my family, I love you. I am forever grateful for your love and support. To my late mother, Katie Brundidge, thank you for showing me what love is. To my late father, Roscoe Brundidge, Sr., thank you for showing me at an early age how to be strong and responsible. To my son, DeSean, whom I love dearly, thank you for showing me that we have a right to enjoy life to the fullest.

Thank you to my pastor, Bishop Edgar Vann II of Second Ebenezer Church, for praying for me and preparing me to go forth and be everything God intended for me to be.

I am grateful for your guidance and instruction. It is because of your leadership, I am who I am today.

To Elder Luevena Dawson, my mentor: For so many years, you have given unselfishly your personal time to pour into me. Words cannot express my complete thanks to you. Thank you for teaching me how to walk in honesty and integrity. Thank you for sharing with me the importance of knowing the word of God.

To my first lady, Elder Shelia Vann: Thank you for showing me what a true woman of excellence is. Thank you for showing me how to carry myself and how to present myself in front of God's people. I thank you for showing me that true anointing comes from being in right standing with God.

My prayer for everyone is that God will continue to bless and prosper you. I pray that he will continue to give you the tools needed to complete His kingdom assignment.

~Elder Kay F. Brundidge

FOREWORD

God has given us one of His most precious gifts in the Body of Christ in the servanthood of *Elder Kay Brundidge.* She has a heart for God that is wholly expressed as a dynamic preacher, missionary, teacher, intercessor, mentor, radio host, and now a prolific writer who will bless many with her Godly wisdom and teaching. It is no secret in the Christian community that she has been set apart as a true general in God's army. She has been faithful and true to her assignments, so much that she is intentional in reaching others for salvation and the edification of the Kingdom of God.

Elder Brundidge aides in co-laboring in

the redemptive and restorative work for God which she shares in this dismal world. This phenomenal book is outlined and saturated with prayer. It overflows with Godly principles and tools which will assist all who may be struggling in moving forward to make a commitment to God's divine direction and purpose for their lives. Be encouraged as God's Word speaks truth and destiny over your life, for you will discover His love and the dynamic plans that He has for you. Get ready to be reignited and rediscover your profound and renewed commitment to God. It will be transformational!

~Elder Renee Welch

CONTENTS

INTRODUCTION

As people on this earth with purpose attached to our lives, we have been called out to make a difference in the world. Our world needs something or somebody they can look to for a brighter pathway.

In this book, you will be introduced to principles that will help you become more true and faithful to what you have been called by God to accomplish. When we understand our purpose, it positions us to be more effective in imparting the lives of others.

Each of us has purpose attached to our lives. Some will seek to search out their purpose, others will not. If you have chosen to fulfill your purpose, this book will give you the necessary tools to succeed. You will learn why it is important to surrender yourself to God.

First Corinthians 2:9 says, *"But as it is written, Eye hath not seen, nor ear heard, neither have entered into the heart of man, the things which God hath prepared for them that love him."* God has great things in store for those who will follow him. On a daily basis, God has been gracious to us; therefore, we owe it to him to be all he has called us to be.

This book will share the importance of walking in the integrity of God, teaching us to be true, and be counted as trustworthy people. Honesty and integrity will have the greatest impact in our world, allowing us to leave a legacy that will impact generations to come.

~Elder Kay Brundidge

CHAPTER ONE:

WHAT SHALL I RENDER?

One day while I sat by the water, I began to think about how good the Lord has been to me. I thought about the many times God has brought me through difficult situations and how many times God made a way of escape for me. On that day, I reflected on how awesome God continues to be in our lives. While sitting there under a large tree, I felt the beautiful summer breeze and listened to the rustling of the leaves. While looking at the waves in the water moving along, there was a calmness about the water. I could appreciate the peace that only God gives to us. All that we are and all that we do only comes by the grace of God. There is a place in God that allows us to receive his peace.

As I took in the beauty of God's creation, the birds chirped in song, as if they were giving praises unto God. I watched the birds moving about looking for food. I was reminded that if God can take care of a little sparrow, surely he can take care of me. I couldn't help but think about what I could do to let God know how much I love and appreciate all he has done for me. What could I surrender to God? I needed to let God know I was available to him and that he could count on me.

I realized that day I would allow God to prepare me to be all he wanted me to be. When we say yes to the will of God, it is an indication to God we understand there is purpose attached to our lives. I knew that day that God has a plan for each of our lives, and I knew I wanted to be a part of his plan. In a time of uncertainty when it appears that people everywhere are seeking to know the mission for their life, when we begin to trust God, that's when he shows us his plan. He is ready to receive us as his own.

"Trust in the Lord with all thine heart; and lean not unto thine own understanding. In all thy ways acknowledge him, and he shall direct thy paths." **Proverbs 3:5-6**

We have been created in the image of God. God wants to shape and mold us, so he may establish us to fulfill his purpose. We have been called out to lead others to Christ. We are called out in such a way that draws others to the love of God and brings glory to God. The closer we allow ourselves to get to God, the more he teaches us who we are in him.

We have been called out by God to be his ambassadors in the earth realm. The world needs to know there are true men and women of God they can trust to show them a better way. The question is can God count on you?

As I wondered about what I could surrender to God, I wondered what it would take to position myself for his process. The process is not always easy, but as we continue to trust God, he gives us the ability to submit to the process. We are living in a time now where people desire to have things quickly. We must understand that God must prepare us for what he has assigned to us. There is a time of preparation that will prove us to be faithful.

"Only fear the Lord, and serve him in truth with all your heart; for consider how great things he hath done for you." **1 Samuel 12:24**

As we submit ourselves for process and preparation, these are principles that will help us on our Christian journey.

1. We must know what it is God has called us to and his will for our lives. God has designed specific things for each of us. We must study the word of God to know him and his will.

"Study to shew thyself approved unto God, a workman that needeth not to be ashamed, rightly dividing the word of truth." **2 Timothy 2:15**

2. If we are going to get closer to God, we must be willing to spend time with God. Every good relationship develops from the time we invest in it. Prayer is the key that puts us in right standing with God. Prayer draws us closer to God and positions us to hear his voice.

"My sheep hear my voice, and I know them, and they follow me:" **John 10:27**

Jesus is our greatest example of a prayer warrior. Many times, the Bible says he would retire to pray to the father.

"And it came to pass in those days, that he went out into a mountain to pray, and continued all night in prayer to God." **Luke 6:12**

Prayer is the one thing that gets the attention of God. He inclines his ear to hear our prayers. When we pray, God makes things happen for our good. The more we pray, the more we can hear from God.

3.　　When we thank God, we honor him. We must always be willing to give God thanks.

"But thanks be to God, which giveth us the victory through our Lord Jesus Christ." **1 Corinthians 15:57**

"In every thing give thanks: for this is the will of God in Christ Jesus concerning you."

1 Thessalonians 5:18

4. We are called to live holy, and put off all ungodly behavior. We must live worthy of our calling. As Christians, we cannot do everything the world does. We have agreed with God to be set apart for his glory, not ours. We must be careful that we don't allow others to rob us from what God has planned for our lives. We must be willing to live as unto God and not man. We must always remember God gets glory when we live as unto the Lord.

"Teaching us that, denying ungodliness and worldly lusts, we should live soberly, righteously, and godly, in this present world." **Titus 2:12**

5. We are called to be God's examples. Being transformed and renewed in our minds; not conforming to the things of this world, but new to godly living.

"I BESEECH you therefore, brethren, by the mercies of God, that ye present your bodies a living sacrifice, holy, acceptable unto God, which is your reasonable service. And be not conformed to this world; but be ye transformed by the renewing of your mind, that ye may prove what is that good, and acceptable, and perfect, will of God." **Romans 12:1-2**

That day, I decided I would surrender all to God. When we come to God as we are, he is willing to accept us as we are. I wanted God to know I was available to him. Today is a good day to surrender all to God.

Let's pray:

Heavenly Father, today we surrender all to you. You are the God of all seasons; thank you for allowing us to be a part of your marvelous plan. We receive all that you have in store for our lives. We know that with you, better things are in store for our future. Amen.

CHAPTER TWO:

EMBRACING GOD'S LOVE

As I continued to gaze at the water, I reflected upon the awesomeness of God. What a calmness I felt, sitting in the presence of God, knowing that only a sovereign God could love us so much. He is a God of unconditional love; he loves us regardless of who we are or what we have gone through.

"For God so loved the world, that he gave his only begotten Son, that whosoever believeth in him should not perish, but have everlasting life."
John 3:16

As I sat there embracing the love of God, I was reassured in my spirit that whatever we are facing, God is more than able to handle what we go through.

"GOD IS our refuge and strength, a very present help in trouble." **Psalm 46:1**

It is because he loves us so much, he commands us to love one another. As Christians, the love we have for one another brings glory to God.

"A new commandment I give unto you, That ye love one another: as I have loved you, that ye also love one another. By this shall all men know that ye are my disciples, if ye have love one to another." **John 13:34-35**

As people of God, we know that everything surrounds the magnificence of God. We know it's never about us, but always about God. As we seek to portray the attributes of God, we allow ourselves to line up with the will of God.

Ask yourself, *what is the will of God, and how do I get in line with his will for my life?*

It is important as Christians to seek out the answers to these questions in order to be in right standing with God.

There are several characteristics that identify the awesomeness of God and his love for us. As we look at these principles, let us be reminded we are here to walk in the ways of God.

1. To know him, we must first know the ultimate sacrifice he made for us: giving his

only begotten Son to die on the cross for our sins that we might be saved from sin (John 3:16).

2. We must be willing to receive him as our Lord and Savior because of what he did for us. We acknowledge that we are sinners and cannot save ourselves (Romans 10:9).

3. Trust in Him. God wants us to trust him in every facet of our lives. God loves when we trust in him. He does his best work after we have exhausted all our resources. He is waiting for us to just rest in him.

We may not always know what God is doing in our lives, but if we can trust him, even when we cannot trace him, he promises through his word that he will never leave us nor forsake us. What an awesome thing to be able to turn everything over to God.

"Casting all your care upon him; for he careth for you." **1 Peter 5:7**

4. Believe God for his blessings. When we receive the love of God, we realize he has already made provisions for us to be blessed. What we need, God will always provide. Our strength comes from God. When we receive God's love, we receive God's power.

"Ye are of God, little children, and have overcome them: because greater is he that is in you, than he that is in the world." **1 John 4:4**

Let us embrace the love of God, and receive his abundant life.

Let us pray:

Father God, you are the one we exalt on high. Teach us how to always give you the glory in every situation. We give thanks to you for your love toward us. Teach us to love one another as you love us. In Jesus' name. Amen.

CHAPTER THREE:

PATIENTLY WAITING ON GOD

"But they that wait upon the Lord shall renew their strength; they shall mount up with wings as eagles; they shall run, and not be weary; and they shall walk, and not faint."
Isaiah 40:31

When we say yes to the will of God, it is an indication to God that we realize we are here for his purpose. We are living in a time now where it appears that the world is moving at a fast pace. Because of our human nature, the circumstances we face can sometimes be overwhelming. In Isaiah 40:31, the prophet Isaiah helps us to know that we can always wait on God even when we don't see his manifestation. God yet assures us he will renew our strength.

God has benefits for those who will wait on him. He says in his word that we will mount up with wings as eagles. When we look at the eagle, it is a very strong bird that shows leadership and authority. The eagle demonstrates power and strength. When we get weak, but continue to wait on God, his power strengthens us.

We may not know what lies ahead, but we know who controls the future. God is a sovereign God; he is ruler of the universe. Trusting God reassures us that he is able to see us through.

Patience is a virtue. We must obtain patience to wait on God. Sometimes, we may get concerned about the circumstances we go through in life, but it takes our faith to wait on God to make everything right. He knows exactly what to do and when to do it. We need to trust God in every aspect of our lives. Sometimes while waiting on God, we become anxious and go ahead of God. We try to handle the situation ourselves instead of waiting on God. When we learn to wait patiently on God, he allows us to rest in him.

God knows all things. Sometimes, God shows us a glimpse of what is to come, but only God knows the proper time of our destiny. He knows the process we must go through in order to be equipped to handle what he gives us. He knows the proper timing. Waiting on God is not always easy, but through prayer and obedience, God teaches us patience. Prayer is the key that draws us closer and connects us with God. Through prayer, we learn to hear the voice of God. When we are connected to him, it makes it easier to obey him.

"Knowing this, that the trying of your faith worketh patience. But let patience have her perfect work, that ye may be perfect and entire, wanting nothing." **James 1:3-4**

God has great things in store for us. We must trust God if we are going to wait on him. God gets the glory when we can trust him, even when we don't always know his plan.

We must continually stay focused and diligent in our kingdom work while waiting on God. All of us have been given the commandment to love one another. While we are in process, we must show the love of God to those in need. There are times when the enemy comes to put obstacles in our pathway to distract us from trusting God, but we must remember that God knows how to stretch our faith, so we may stand in the time of adversity.

We must have such determination that nothing or no one will separate us from the love of God.

"For I am persuaded, that neither death, nor life, nor angels, nor principalities, nor powers, nor things present, nor things to come. Nor height,

nor depth, nor any other creature, shall be able to separate us from the love of God, which is in Christ Jesus our Lord." **Romans 8:38-39**

God gets the glory from our lives when we can remain steadfast and determined to trust him. Steadfast means to be firm and unwavering in purpose. Determine to be loyal to what we have promised God, knowing and believing what God promises to us he will complete.

"Therefore, my beloved brethren, be ye stedfast, unmovable, always abounding in the work the Lord, forasmuch as ye know that your labour is not in vain in the Lord." **1 Corinthians 15:58**

There are times when we will experience tough times and may look to others for help. Have you ever needed help and couldn't tell anyone your problem? This is the exact time God steps in. God has proven to be help in times of trouble. This is when we know God is our strength. He shows us there is nothing he will not do to protect us.

"GOD IS our refuge and strength, a very present help in trouble." **Psalm 46:1**

No matter what we go through God promises to always be with us.

"Let your conversation be without covetousness; and be content with such things as ye have: for he hath said, I will never leave thee, nor forsake thee." **Hebrews 13:5**

I have experienced enough in my life to say I am determined to trust and wait on God, no matter how long it takes. I remember going through a challenge in my life. My home was going into foreclosure. I remember being on the side of my house and hearing the Lord say so clearly, "*They will not take your home. I gave it to you and I will take it away; and when I take it away, I will give you something bigger*". I stood on the promises of God and I knew God would not go back on his word. I had no money to pay my mortgage, but I believed God. Five years later, I am still residing in my home. God makes true to his word. If we can trust God, everything he promises he will make true.

"Let us hold fast the profession of our faith without wavering; (for he is faithful that promised;)" **Hebrews 10:23**

We must hold onto the promises of God. We cannot afford to let circumstances alter our belief in God. The tougher it gets, the more we've got to trust God. The more we wait on God, the easier it becomes to turn everything over to him. He loves us unconditionally, and he waits for us to trust in him. If God says it, he will perform it. If we continue to wait on God and remain patient, he'll bring us peace.

"Rest in the Lord, and wait patiently for him: fret not thyself because of him who prospereth in his way, because of the man who bringeth wicked devices to pass." **Psalm 37:7**

God wants to release blessings to his people as we continue to trust him. He is a God who will not let us down. Sometimes, we put our trust in others, and the outcome is not always good; but when we trust God, he will always make a way for us. The Lord is all knowing; he is well able to bring all things together at the appointed time.

Many times, while waiting on God, we tend to believe prematurely that we are ready for the things God has for us. While God may allow us to get a glimpse of what is to come, only he sees the complete picture. We do well to remember in times like these, God does not have to wait on us, we are waiting on God. When we move ahead of God, he cannot prepare us completely for the journey.

There is a process we must go through for God to approve us as ready to be released for kingdom work. The Lord God takes pleasure when his sons and daughters trust him enough to wait on him.

Let's pray:

Heavenly Father, thank you for teaching us how to wait on you. We know you have great plans for our lives. We will patiently wait on your timing. We believe what you are doing in our lives will bring glory to your Kingdom. We stand in agreement that everything is in divine order. In Jesus' name. Amen.

CHAPTER FOUR:

HOLD ON TO YOUR INTEGRITY

What type of person does God see when he looks at us? Does God see someone who thinks before they speak? Does he see someone he can trust to be faithful with the things of God? God is concerned about how we represent his kingdom. Integrity means everything to God. We must always remember who we are in God and be mindful of our actions. We are living in a time where it appears our integrity is being compromised. What we once held in high regard now seems to carry little value. This is a time the world needs to see men and women who say they know God and walk in value and character. The world needs to see an example of holy men and women of God.

Being a person who is intrigued by the small details of people, I've often noticed that people who are true and honest, although the world may think otherwise, obtain favor with God. It pleases God when we stay true to the right things. It doesn't take much effort now to waiver, but it does take stamina to walk in integrity. Have you ever stopped to think about the people who received favor in everything they put their hands to?

Integrity means the adherence to a code of values. We must hold fast to the principles that line up with God's law. We have been set apart to live a life of holiness and honesty. God wants to count on us to represent him in the kingdom. We are his kingdom ambassadors!

What does God say to us about walking in integrity?

"I BESEECH you therefore, brethren, by the mercies of God, that ye present your bodies a living sacrifice, holy, acceptable unto God, which is your reasonable service."
Romans 12:1

God lays it out for us through his word. We are to present our bodies to be the sacrifice that will draw others to him. Our sacrifice is in the way we talk, how we walk and how we live. It is important as representatives of God, that people see God through us. The world is looking at the body of Christ for guidance. We must present ourselves in a way that will draw others to Christ.

Our integrity speaks of our character. We must allow God to equip us as his servants. It is so important that we understand that we are living in a time when people are compromising on all levels. God must know he can count on his people to be truthful and honest. We must be the example the world needs to see, so they can see God through us. There is a difference between God's standard and the world's standard. God's standard represents excellence and honesty, while the world's standard lacks accountability.

Suppose you are the CEO of a well-known company, and how your employees conduct themselves on and off the job is a reflection to the company. The owner knows if he is to have a reputable business, he must take time to prepare his employees. There is a process and training they must go through in order to be knowledgeable and effective to the company. It is the same with God. God must prepare his people to be empowered ambassadors for the kingdom. There is a process that God must take us through to prepare us for our assignment. You must be willing to walk in ways that please God. If we are to represent God, we must carry the love of God. We must take pride in pleasing God.

Here are some ways in which we can walk in integrity.

1. Seek to be trustworthy. The world needs to know there are still people they can put their trust in. When they need hope, they can be assured through us that we represent a God who still cares for them. We have been called to walk in the integrity of God.

"That you put off concerning the former conversation the old man, which is corrupt according to the deceitful lusts; And be renewed in the spirit of your mind. And that ye put on the new man, which after God is created in righteousness and true holiness."
Ephesians 4:22-24

Christians should desire to live a holy life. We are the examples others can see so they can live a righteous life. We must be willing to put away our old behaviors that prohibit us from bringing glory to God. Are you willing to go the distance with God that he may prove you trustworthy?

2. A willingness to be obedient to God. It is our obedience that gets God's attention. God rewards those who are obedient to him. God looks at obedience as being greater than our sacrifice. It is our obedience that brings on the favor of God.

"If ye be willing and obedient, ye shall eat the good of the land." **Isaiah 1:19**

3. Seek to become closer to God. We are the chosen of God. We must seek to have the heart and mind of God. The closer we get to God, the more we avail ourselves to be used by God.

"Ye have not chosen me, but I have chosen you, and ordained you, that ye should go and bring forth fruit, and that your fruit should remain; that whatsoever ye shall ask of the Father in my name, he may give it you." **John 15:16**

When we are in position to be used by God, we can receive from God. We are the light of the world, being guided by the Holy Spirit to represent God in dark places. When we have the proper light, we can overshadow the dark things in this world.

"But if we walk in the light, as he is in the light, we have fellowship one with another, and the blood of Jesus Christ his Son cleanseth us from all sin." **1 John 1:7**

Walking in the integrity of God starts with the renewing of your mind. We must first believe we are new creatures in Christ. Transformation begins in our mind. We must possess a life of integrity in our hearts. God is always concerned about the heart of man.

"But the Lord said unto Samuel, Look not on his countenance, or on the height of his stature; because I have refused him: for the Lord seeth not as man seeth; for man looketh on the outward appearance, but the Lord looketh on the heart."
1 Samuel 16:7

Having integrity allows us to be mindful of the things in our hearts. We must be willing to do a self-examination to purge out that which bears bad fruit.

"Search me, O God, and know my heart: try me, and know my thoughts: And see if there be any

wicked way in me, and lead me in the way everlasting." **Psalm 139:23-24**

God gives favor to the person who walks in integrity. A person of integrity will always strive to walk in honesty. A person of integrity knows that their life represents the fact that they can be trusted of men, therefore being trusted by God. They know this is what God expects from us. Are you that person God can offer up just as he did with Job, and knows without a doubt you will not let him down?

Let's pray:

Heavenly Father, thank you for showing us how to walk in integrity. Lord, we understand to be honest and true represents all that you are. Help us Lord not to conform to the ways of this world, but always being conscious of the things that please you. In Jesus' name. Amen.

CHAPTER FIVE:

WALKING IN THE FAITH OF GOD

One thing that brings us closer to God is the ability to walk in faith, even when we are not always sure what God is doing in our lives.

Faith allows us to believe God despite what we may be going through. Sometimes, God will allow circumstances to arise in our lives to see how much we will trust him. The things we go through only help to strengthen our faith in God. God wants to mature us to a level in him that no matter what things appear to be, he is a faithful and a just God who will never let us down.

"For the word of the Lord is right; and all his works are done in truth." **Psalm 33:4**

We must come to a place in our spiritual walk where we must believe God at any cost and take him at his word. Faith in God allows us to know who God is, and what he can do to us and through us. Faith is the key that allows us to receive an abundant life in God.

"NOW FAITH is the substance of things hoped for, the evidence of things not seen." **Hebrews 11:1**

If we are going to get to a place of believing God, hoping for what is not seen yet, we must give God access to our lives. There are many things God must do in us in order to work through us. Because his thoughts and ways are higher than ours, he sees things in us that we cannot see, even those things that must be purged from us, so we can be effective in kingdom work.

We may not see it yet, but at the appointed time, God will bring it to pass. It is when he has tried us and proven us to be faithful and trustworthy that he brings us forth to complete the destiny he has on our lives.

As Christians, our assignment is to fulfill the mandate God has placed on our lives in the earth realm. We are to spread the gospel of Jesus, ultimately drawing others to Christ. We must always be willing to teach others to put their trust in God and let the world know all things are possible with God.

Faith is resilience under pressure. It is the ability to trust God, even when he is not traceable. Have you ever been in a situation where nothing worked for you, and the only thing that would help you out was to believe God for a miracle? Just know that God is a miracle worker; nothing is too hard for God.

Faith commands us to be steadfast and unmovable. We must be willing to return to our original position of trusting God at all times, always remembering that our destiny is tied to God's purpose for our lives. When we are steadfast to the trials we go through, it allows God to strengthen our testimonies. If you know that God brought you out once, you have already been reassured that he can do it again. What better way to witness when we ourselves have been brought through by our precious Lord and Savior Jesus Christ!

Here are some principles that will help you walk in the faith of God:

1. Study the word of God. When we study God's word, it draws us closer to God. The more we know about him, the more we can learn what his will is for our lives. God's word teaches us his unconditional love for us, and how we are to love one another. It is in his word we see the will of God. God has commanded us to study the word of God. It is through the word of God we are equipped to do the work of the Lord. His word lets us know that being connected to God brings on the blessings of God. When we know that it is God's will that we prosper, we are assured

through faith to receive everything God promises.

"The thief cometh not, but for to steal, and to kill, and to destroy: I am come that they might have life, and that they might have it more abundantly." **John 10:10**

2. Persistent in Prayer. When we spend time in prayer, we can make our petitions known unto God and yet, we can hear his voice as he speaks to us. It is prayer that ultimately connects us to God in ways that we cannot imagine. Prayer builds our relationship with God. It is effective prayer that makes the difference in the lives of God's people. Being persistent in prayer allows you to pray daily, knowing the joy of being in his presence. Prayer will cause you to trust God until you

see results. When you seek God in prayer every morning, he guides you throughout the day.

"My voice shalt thou hear in the morning, O Lord; in the morning will I direct my prayer unto thee, and will look up." **Psalm 5:3**

3. Fellowship with other Christians. When we connect with other Christians, we strengthen one another. A unit of believers can do great work in the kingdom of God. When we stand together in strength, we can block the attack of the enemy. We are one body joined together to encourage each other, while together we encourage others to trust God. We are a family of believers who God needs to show the world what family unity

looks like. We show others what it means when families are reconciled.

"Be kindly affectioned one to another with brotherly love; in honour preferring one another" **Romans 12:10**

We cannot even imagine the things God has in store for those who walk in faith. The favor of God rests on our lives when we walk in faith.

"But as it is written, Eye hath not seen, nor ear heard, neither have entered into the heart of man, the things which God hath prepared for them that love him." **1 Corinthians 2:9**

What are the benefits of walking in faith?

1. Faith will bring salvation. It is through saving faith we have a right to receive

Jesus as our Lord and Savior. Believing that God sent his Son to die on the cross for our sins, repenting of our sins and confessing that we believe Jesus died and rose with all power, allows us to receive eternal life.

"That if thou shalt confess with thy mouth the Lord Jesus, and shalt believe in thine heart that God hath raised him from the dead, thou shalt be saved." **Romans 10:9**

2. Faith causes prayers to be answered. When we pray, believing that God will answer our prayers, it moves the heart of God. God has given to everyone a measure of faith. When we believe God, and take him at his word, it puts us in position to receive, according to his will,

the things we ask for in prayer. God promises that when we pray, he will hear us and answer our prayers. Whatever it is you believe God for, through your faith in God, he is able to answer your prayer.

"And this is the confidence that we have in him, that, if we ask any thing according to his will, he heareth us: And if we know that he hear us, whatsoever we ask, we know that we have the petitions that we desired of him." **1 John 5:14-15**

3. Faith allows God to use us greatly. It is because God has purpose attached to our lives; he has already placed destiny over our lives. When we submit ourselves to God, trusting him for his direction, he can prepare us for a great work in the kingdom. God

needs those that will represent him in the earth realm. We are his ambassadors, called out to spread the gospel of Jesus.

"Go ye therefore, and teach all nations, baptizing them in the name of the Father, and of the Son, and of the Holy Ghost: Teaching them to observe all things whatsoever I have commanded you: and, lo, I am with you always, even unto the end of the world. Amen." **Matthew 28:19-20**

4. Faith brings healing. God is a healer. In the word of God, we see that through faith, many were healed. It is not the will of God that we suffer illness and not allow him to perform healing in our lives. He wants us healed, delivered and made whole. If you can trust God for your healing, you can receive God's healing power.

"O LORD my God, I cried unto thee, and thou hast healed me." **Psalm 30:2**

5. Faith brings the peace of God. When we understand that God is a peacemaker, he is the one who gives us ultimate peace. Many people try to obtain peace in various ways, which may only be temporal. There is a peace that only God can give when we are connected to him. In our world today, where many things going on bring on a spirit of anxiety, the world needs to know that through faith in God, he gives us a peace that passes all understanding. He gives us a peace that overshadows any situation we go through. When we put our faith in God, he blesses us with his peace. God is peace; when we connect with him, we walk in the spirit of his peace.

"And the peace of God, which passeth all understanding, shall keep your hearts and minds through Christ Jesus." **Philippians 4:7**

God is so true to his word that he expects us to be true to what we do. It is our faith and trust in God that says we believe him to be a sovereign God. Faith in God is the answer to every prayer. When we know God to be the Almighty One, we will rejoice in the things of God, knowing that all good things come from God.

"For the Lord God is a sun and shield; the Lord will give grace and glory; no good thing will he withhold from them that walk uprightly."

Psalm 84:11

Let's pray:

Heavenly Father, thank you for teaching us how to walk in faith. We know that trusting you makes everything worth waiting for. Thank you for being a God that can be trusted at all times, thank you for never leaving us. In Jesus' name. Amen.

CHAPTER SIX:

MY OBEDIENCE TO GOD

Have you ever wondered why obedience is so important to God? Obedience places us in right standing with God. It allows God to know who can be trusted by him. Webster defines obedience as *to be in compliance with an order, or request, the submission to another's authority.* True obedience positions us to be used by God.

God takes pleasure in our obedience to his commandments. When we commit to obey God, we become the children of God. The greatest commandment he leaves with us is to love one another as he loves us.

God's love for us is unconditional. Even in challenging times when it may seem we have lost our way, God never turns his back on us. He loves us no matter who we are, or what we have been through. There are times when we may feel alone, believing that no one cares. It is at our lowest times when God will reach out to draw us to his love. It was the love of God that caused him to give his only begotten Son to die on the cross that we might have eternal life.

"For God so loved the world, that he gave his only begotten Son, that whosoever believeth in him should not perish, but have everlasting life."
John 3:16

As people of God, the more we connect to God, the more we demonstrate the characteristics of God. We obey him because we believe in him. Obedience is the key to our relationship with God. If we are to be followers of Christ, we must follow his example in obeying God. Jesus fulfilled his assignment to obey God by his death on the cross for all mankind. We obey God because we love him.

Here are some principles to help us become more obedient to God:

1. Trustworthy. God wants to release his plan in the earth realm. It is his will that none should be lost. If we are to be the examples God is looking for to let a dying world know he saves, we must present ourselves holy and righteous. As followers of Christ, we are obligated to obey the commands of God.

Whatever God has gifted us to do, we must do it to the glory of God. We may not have the same gifts, but we must remain committed to the gifts God has given us. The more the Lord can count on us, the more he is able to use us to show his love.

"And I thank Christ Jesus our Lord, who hath enabled me, for that he counted me faithful, putting me into the ministry." **1 Timothy 1:12**

2. Humility. We are living in a time where we are witnessing much selfishness in our world. The Bible speaks of a time when men will be puffed up and lovers of themselves. Jesus comes into the world as the Son of God, yet the Bible lets us know he is as humble as a lamb. When we understand that all glory belongs to God, it makes it easy for us to

humble ourselves before God. If we are going to exalt the name of Jesus, we must humble ourselves as servants of the Most High King. Never lifting ourselves up, but knowing it is because of God we have been chosen by him.

"Humble yourselves therefore under the mighty hand of God, that he may exalt you in due time:"
1 Peter 5:6

3. Loving. The ultimate love is the demonstration of God's love toward us. God loves us so much, he is able to forgive our sins and receive us as his own. We must be willing to show the love of God in all that we do. Love must be the root of our kingdom work. God's greatest commandment is that we love him first, and love one another as he loves us.

"Beloved, let us love one another: for love is of God; and every one that loveth is born of God, and knoweth God. He that loveth not knoweth not God; for God is love."
1 John 4:7-8

Our obedience to God represents our walk with God. We are God's ambassadors in the earth. We have been assigned by God to be on the front line to bring peace to the world. We walk in the ministry of reconciliation. We are the mouthpiece of God, lifting up his name throughout the world.

"And I, if I be lifted up from the earth, will draw all men unto me." **John 12:32**

Effective Obedience

1. When we abide in God, and his words abide in us, we establish a relationship with God. It is through our relationship with God, others can be saved.

2. Our obedience to God is the demonstration of our love for God. We love him, and we obey him.

3. Our sincere obedience assures God we can be trusted to fulfill his assignments. It is wonderful to be counted trustworthy to fulfill our assignment to God, spreading the word of God around the world that others will know him in the pardon of their sins.

4. Going through the process equips us to lead others to Christ.

5. We are able to serve others with excellence. God is an excellent God. Submitting to God puts us in position to serve God's people in love.

6. We must remain focused and committed to our God-given assignment. We cannot become distracted; we must remain steadfast to the work of ministry.

We must continue showing our love for God. Being obedient to God makes us ready to lead others to the love of God. When we understand the mandate God has given to us, we are clear about our commitment to God. It is an honor to be used by the Most High King.

Let's pray:

Lord, thank you for showing us how important our obedience is to you. Teach us to obey you at all times, never leaning to our own understanding, but always trusting you and obeying you. Amen.

CHAPTER SEVEN:

THE FAVOR OF GOD

When I think of how great it is to walk in the favor of God, nothing compares to his favor. Only when God can trust us, it brings on great blessings. When we walk in the favor of God, we can remain at peace even when things are unfavorable, knowing that, somehow, God works things out for our good.

What an amazing blessing it is to know that God would favor his sons and daughters who live true to his word. When we are connected to God, no matter what we go through, God will sustain us.

Have you ever had to meet a deadline and did not know how that would happen? You knew that it would take a miracle to accomplish this task. You had no idea where to turn. God stepped into your situation and brought favor to your circumstance. It *is your testimony today that it was only the favor of God that brought you through.* God knows exactly what we need and when we need it. He can change the entire dynamic of a situation just to meet our needs.

"But my God shall supply all your need according to his riches in glory by Christ Jesus."
Philippians 4:19

Let us explore some benefits of walking in the favor of God.

1. Walking in the favor of God produces increase. When we submit to God's process for our lives, we give permission for the Holy Spirit to usher us into the deeper things of God. We increase in wisdom and understanding. The favor of God brings the abundant life in God. The favor of God will allow us to receive the things we did not plan for.

"The Lord shall increase you more and more, you and your children." **Psalm 115:14**

2. Favor brings victory. It is God's will for us to prosper. Connecting ourselves properly with God puts us in alignment to receive the victory of God. We are victorious in God, and not defeated. Victory belongs to the people of God. We have been redeemed by Jesus

Christ. We are protected by the power of God. When we are victorious, we know who we are in God. I am who God says I am.

"Now thanks be unto God, which always causeth us to triumph in Christ, and maketh manifest the savour of his knowledge by us in every place." **2 Corinthians 2:14**

3. Favor in God opens doors. God has a prepared destiny over our lives. Our destiny was preordained by God. He already knew the plans for our lives before we entered our mothers' wombs.

"For I know the thoughts that I think toward you, saith the Lord, thoughts of peace, and not of evil, to give you an expected end." **Jeremiah 29:11**

4. Favor brings God's protection and provision. God covers us daily. He knows our needs at all times. He is the great provider who covers us with his protection. He blocks the attack of the enemy. He protects us from danger, seen and unseen. He is omnipresent; he's everywhere at the same time. Because he is a sovereign God, he is in control of all things, at all times.

"For thou, Lord, wilt bless the righteous; with favour wilt thou compass him as with a shield."
Psalm 5:12

"The name of the Lord is a strong tower: the righteous runneth into it, and is safe."
Proverbs 18:10

We know that God is true to his word; whatever he says he will perform it. Those who seek after the things of God will receive the glory of God. God is waiting on those who will surrender to his will and be the examples he needs to carry the message of salvation.

When we walk upright and in integrity, we attract others to the knowledge of God. God must become a priority in our lives, so others may know him. Trust God for the things he has in store for you. God has prepared greater for his people.

Let's pray:

Father God, thank you for favor on our lives. Teach us to desire your favor daily, help us to know we have a right to receive the blessings of God. We have a right to walk in the favor of God. Amen.

CHAPTER EIGHT:

REMAINING COMMITTED

Our willingness to remain committed to the things of God allows God to trust us and position us for greatness.

Webster defines commitment as *being dedicated to a specific cause*. As Christians, we should be committed to spreading the gospel of Jesus, and being obedient to his commandments. Faithfulness to the will of God brings on the willingness to obey God. It is not always easy to remain committed, but God is faithful to give us what we need when we need it. We must continue to trust him for guidance.

In challenging times, when it seems hard to remain committed, this is the very time we should reach for the word of God. Even in our weakest times, God will surely give us what we need.

"Trust in the Lord with all thine heart; and lean not unto thine own understanding. In all thy ways acknowledge him, and he shall direct thy paths." **Proverbs 3:5-6**

"He giveth power to the faint; and to them that have no might he increaseth strength." **Isaiah 40:29**

Faithfulness is a key factor to the Christian life. We are clear that without faith, we cannot please God.

"But without faith it is impossible to please him; for he that cometh to God must believe that he is, and that he is a rewarder of them that diligently seek him." **Hebrews 11:6**

In times of uncertainty, our faith in God gives us the peace of God. It is what he has promised to us. When we carry the peace of God, we can remain committed to God and rest in God knowing that his peace will cover us.

"Peace I leave with you, my peace I give unto you; not as the world giveth, give I unto you. Let not your heart be troubled, neither let it be afraid." **John 14:27**

Principles to help us remain committed:

Knowing the character of God: When we have studied the character of God and are willing to duplicate his characteristics, we can then walk in the knowledge of God. God's character is love. He has unconditional love for us. When we take on his nature of love, we can love him and love others.

His character is strength: Moving in the strength of God allows us to be strong in the Lord. It is God who we lean and depend upon to carry us through. God strengthens us with his power.

"Fear thou not; for I am with thee: be not dismayed; for I am thy God: I will strengthen thee; yea, I will help thee; yea, I will uphold thee with the right hand of my righteousness."
Isaiah 41:10

God's character is forgiving: God forgave us when he redeemed us. We were born into sin. It is the blood of Jesus that washes away our sins. We have been forgiven and made free. As believers of Christ, we too must be willing to forgive others of their transgressions. When we cannot forgive others, God will not forgive our sins.

"And when ye stand praying, forgive, if ye have aught against any: that your Father also which is in heaven may forgive you your trespasses." **Mark 11:25**

Spending time in God's presence: When we spend time in the presence of God, we build a relationship with God. It is in his presence we receive the joy of the Lord. His presence blocks out the enemy and takes us to a place the enemy cannot enter. When we spend time in prayer, we begin to recognize God's voice. We can hear and obey him. When we spend time in his presence, the glory of God overshadows us. Nothing compares to his glory. In his presence, God covers us; his compassion soothes our very soul. Being able to worship God brings glory to him, and heals whatever we go through.

"O God, thou art my God; early will I seek thee: my soul thirsteth for thee, my flesh longeth for thee in a dry and thirsty land, where no water is; To see thy power and thy glory, so as I have seen thee in the sanctuary." **Psalm 63:1-2**

Study the word of God: 2 Timothy 2:15 says, *"Study to shew thyself approved unto God, a workman that needeth not to be ashamed, rightly* *dividing the word of truth."* It is the commandment of God that we study his word. We are his representatives here on earth. We are to be ready to share the word of God with others at all times, that they may know him in the pardon of their sins. When we study his word, we learn the will of God for our lives. God has a set destiny for each of our lives.

God has benefits for those who remain committed:

1. **Strengthening our relationship with God.** The greatest relationship we can have is the one with Jesus Christ. We learn about relationships with others at an early age. We learn that a family relationship strengthens us, and teaches

us how to pull together as a family. There are times when we experience good relationships and other times, not so good. When we come into relationship with Jesus Christ, nothing remains the same. We become new in Christ. Our old behaviors change, and we take on a better way of living. Having a relationship with Jesus brings the joy of the Lord into our lives.

2. **Growing in grace.** It is a great benefit to grow in the grace of God. It is his unmerited favor that covers us. When you walk in his grace, God opens doors that no man can shut. The doors he needs to shut no one can open. The grace of God sustains us in challenging

times. What we go through prepares us for our divine destiny. No matter what things look like, God's grace is sufficient for us.

3. **Walking in the Spirit of God.** Walking in the Spirit of God allows us to display the love of God. It is God's Spirit that directs and guides us daily. Through the leading of his spirit, we receive discernment. His spirit protects us from danger. When we move in the spirit of God, it draws others to God. People are drawn to the right spirit. God's Spirit will cause us to walk in the joy of the Lord, that others can restore their joy by their connection with us. In a world of darkness, people need to see the light of

Christ. The peace of God moves within us. We are able to stand in his peace no matter what is happening around us.

4. **Abundant life.** Christ came that we would have abundant life. It is the will of God that we prosper. We cannot imagine the great things God has already promised to us. If we can remain committed to God, even if we don't see it in the natural as of yet, we can be assured it will manifest at the appointed time. God will do just what he says. He is true to his promise.

"Being confident of this very thing, that he which hath begun a good work in you will perform it until the day of Jesus Christ." **Philippians 1:6**

God has much work to be done. Staying committed allows us to fulfill the mandate on our lives. It positions us to serve in ways that gives God the glory. We must never allow any circumstance to distract us from giving God our best. He is looking for those who will be effective in the kingdom work.

"Therefore, my beloved brethren, be ye stedfast, unmoveable, always abounding in the work of the Lord, forasmuch as ye know that your labour is not in vain in the Lord."
1 Corinthians 15:58

We have victory in God and the enemy is already defeated. We can rejoice in Jesus, who has made us free. God has commanded us to be planted in the work of the Lord, and not easily moved. When we remain committed to kingdom work, the labor we sacrifice will not be in vain. God will not forget our labor.

Let's pray:

Father God, we thank you for allowing us to work in your vineyard. Teach us not to be easily moved. Strengthen us to remain faithful and committed to the work of the ministry. Amen.

CHAPTER NINE:

DETERMINED TO MOVE FORWARD

When we choose to move forward in God, we make a conscious decision that no matter what we face, we are determined to keep moving. God is a progressive God who keeps moving. It is only when we connect ourselves to God that we realize that everything we need is in God.

You cannot encounter God and remain the same. It is when we get connected to Christ that we take on a newness in him. The old behavior and old attitude begins to change. The things we used to find ourselves doing, we can no longer do. Something begins to change inside of us. It is our priority to be more pleasing to God.

"Therefore if any man be in Christ, he is a new creature: old things are passed away; behold, all things are become new." **2 Corinthians 5:17**

Moving forward allows you to see yourself as God sees you. God has purpose attached to each of our lives, and it is his intended desire to see us prosper.

Principles that will help you move forward:

1. Persistent in prayer.

Prayer is the key that allows us to speak to God, and listen as he speaks to us. Prayer will draw us closer to God. We must be willing to pray daily, thanking

God for who he is, and what he continues to do to us and through us.

"My voice shalt thou hear in the morning, O Lord; in the morning will I direct my prayer unto thee, and will look up." **Psalm 5:3**

When we are determined to move forward, we recognize the importance of starting our day with God. Acknowledge God at the beginning of the day, and seek to be in right standing with him.

"But seek ye first the kingdom of God, and his righteousness; and all these things shall be added unto you." **Matthew 6:33**

2. We must be rooted and grounded in God to move forward

When we are rooted and grounded in God, we become steadfast and unmovable. When we become grounded in God, the enemy cannot uproot us. No matter what you face, you can continue to trust God at all costs. God's promise is he will never leave us nor forsake us.

"Let your conversation be without covetousness; and be content with such things as ye have: for he hath said, I will never leave thee, nor forsake thee." **Hebrews 13:5**

Being rooted in God allows us to shake off those things that so easily try to beset us. When we are rooted and grounded in God, we stand firm against the wiles of the devil. We can make a conscious decision to stay with God.

3. Committed to follow the direction of
   God

   When we are moving forward in God,
   we must be careful not to listen to
   direction that does not line up with the
   will of God. Many people believe all
   sorts of things today; however, you
   must be clear on the word of God and
   stand firm on your beliefs.

*"Trust in the Lord with all thine heart; and lean
not unto thine own understanding. In all thy
ways acknowledge him, and he shall direct thy
paths."* **Proverbs 3:5-6**

   Moving forward says to me, I may not
   always know what God is doing in my
   life, but I will trust in him to work it out.
   Knowing that his ways and his thoughts

are much higher than ours, we acknowledge him in everything we do, believing he will show us the right pathway.

4. Knowing who you are in God

It is important to know who you are in God. If you are unsure about your identity in God, you cannot be clear about what or who you are following. When you are clear on your identity in God, it makes it hard for others to distract you from God's intended purpose for your life. You must be convinced that you are victorious in God. You know that God has purpose attached to your life. We are victorious because we have been bought with a price. Jesus has already paid the price on Calvary.

The following are declarations that we can speak over ourselves:

"I can do all things through Christ which strengtheneth me." **Philippians 4:13**

"But know that the LORD hath set apart him that is godly for himself; the LORD will hear when I call unto him." **Psalm 4:3**

"Now unto him that is able to do exceeding abundantly above all that we ask or think, according to the power that worketh in us." **Ephesians 3:20**

"Strengthened with all might, according to his glorious power, unto all patience and longsuffering with joyfulness;" **Colossians 1:11**

"Blessed be the Lord, who daily loadeth us with benefits, even the God of our salvation. Selah."
Psalm 68:19

There are times in our lives when we may encounter stumbling blocks. These are times we must press forward through tough times, knowing that God is still in control. Even when it seems like we are alone, we press through with a determination to keep moving forward in God. We are called to make a difference in the lives of others. We are called to show them that through God, there is a better way to live. The greatest thing we can do as Christians is to bring hope to those in need. If we are the ones to bring hope in this world, we must not quit. As we continue to move forward, others can receive Christ.

"Let us hold fast the profession of our faith without wavering; (for he is faithful that promised;)" **Hebrews 10:23**

Let's pray:

Father God, we thank you for allowing us to move forward in you. You are a God that will not let us down. Help us to be all you have called us to be, that we may continue to give you glory. Amen.

CONCLUSION

We have learned the importance of being true to the things of God. God rewards faithfulness and honesty. It is the truth within us that allows others to see the purity in God. We represent a God who cares.

In a world where we are seeing the struggles and challenges people face daily, those of us who say we are followers of Christ must be prepared to show others there is a better way to live. It is our integrity that allows others to trust us enough to see the good in the world and believe God for change in their lives.

We have covered various topics to show us what it means to be true to what we do. In a world where sometimes it is hard to view truth, we are the ones to show through our lives God is still faithful. If we are going to be the ones chosen to make our world better, we must first present ourselves to be properly trained so we can equip others. When we surrender all to God, we position ourselves for God's purpose.

God has destined purpose on each of our lives. He already knows the plans he has set for us. This is why the process is so important. When we position ourselves for God's process, we receive everything needed to complete our assignment. The process is not always easy, but if we can hold out and trust God, we will reap the benefits of God, and bring glory to God.

When we learn to trust God at all costs, we learn to patiently wait on God. I will wait in good times and challenging times, because I know the outcome at the appointed time will be favorable.

My prayer is that you will stay true to what God assigns to you, never wavering, never compromising. You have been given the tools needed to work on the things God wants to strengthen in you. Be satisfied with what God has destined for you, not coveting anyone else's gifts or talents, but knowing what God has for you, it is for you.

ABOUT THE AUTHOR

As a minister and missionary who predicate her ministerial gifts upon Acts 1:8, Elder Kay Brundidge serves faithfully with a heart to reach the lost.

Elder Brundidge's global outreach calling has afforded her the opportunity to minister the gospel in parts of Ukraine, Russia, South Africa and Jamaica.

She is the founder and leader of *Healing for the Soul Ministries*, a charitable outreach ministry designed to bring people into total wholeness in mind, body and soul. Her passion for ministry and her willingness to hear God has positioned her to be greatly used by God throughout the world. As part of her global outreach, Elder Brundidge ministers every Friday on 1440 AM WMKM at 10:45 am EST, reaching thousands by air and millions worldwide online.

Thank you for your purchase of this book. We encourage you to submit a review on www.amazon.com after reading it to share what you gleaned from this book with others.

If you would like to contact the author, you can reach Elder Kay F. Brundidge at BeTrueTheBook@gmail.com for more information.

Made in the USA
Monee, IL
12 April 2022